Incredible Explorers

John Cabot
Searching for a
Westward Passage to Asia

Zachary Anderson

Cavendish
Square

New York

Published in 2015 by Cavendish Square Publishing, LLC
243 5th Avenue, Suite 136, New York, NY 10016

Library of Congress Cataloging-in-Publication Data
Anderson, Zachary.
John Cabot : searching for a westward passage to Asia / Zachary Anderson.
pages cm. — (Incredible explorers)
Includes index.
ISBN 978-1-50260-173-5 (hardcover) ISBN 978-1-50260-172-8 (ebook)
1. Cabot, John, -1498?—Juvenile literature. 2. America—Discovery and exploration—British—Juvenile literature.
3. North America—Discovery and exploration—British—Juvenile literature. 4. Explorers—America—Biography—Juvenile literature. 5. Explorers—Great Britain—Biography—Juvenile literature. 6. Explorers—Italy—Biography—Juvenile literature. I. Title.

E129.C1A53 2015
910.92—dc23
[B]

2014028232

Editor: Andrew Coddington
Copy Editor: Cynthia Roby
Art Director: Jeffrey Talbot
Designer: Douglas Brooks
Photo Researcher: J8 Media
Production Manager: Jennifer Ryder-Talbot
Production Editor: David McNamara

Contents

Introduction

A Mysterious Explorer

John Cabot lived and explored more than 500 years ago, but historians are still trying to create a detailed account of his journeys. They do know that the **Venetian** navigator sailed from Bristol, England, in 1497 under a charter from the King of England. Cabot headed west out on the

Not much is known about the life of John Cabot, the Venetian explorer who sailed for England.

northern Atlantic Ocean, looking to claim land in the New World, or more specifically North America, for England. About fifty days later, Cabot and his crew landed in what is now Canada and claimed the new land for King Henry VII.

This simplified version of Cabot's explorations is also one that historians have painstakingly pieced together from few documents. No shipboard **logs** or diaries have survived to tell us of Cabot's adventure, so scholars have little more than secondhand letters to recount the events of his life. No grave marker remains of Cabot, and few, if any, painted portraits of the explorer hang in any museums. His sons exaggerated his achievements, often enhancing them to gain prestige. Sometimes, Cabot's son Sebastian took the credit for his father's prior voyages. Even historians who recorded events within twenty-five years of Cabot's landfall in the New World had to ask the name of the man who sailed from Bristol during the summer of 1497.

More than five centuries have passed since Cabot's Canadian landing. Some historians have relied on his story to bolster Canada's national pride. Others have strongly argued that Cabot, not Christopher Columbus, was the actual explorer responsible for the "discovery" of North America by Europeans. Columbus (1451–1506) may have sailed across the warmer mid-latitudes of the Atlantic Ocean five years earlier than Cabot, but he landed on the islands of the Caribbean. Not until 1498, a year after Cabot's landfall in Canada, did Columbus reach the mainland of South America. Even Amerigo Vespucci, after whom South America was named in 1507, traveled along the southern continent, but he did not set foot on its mainland until 1497 or 1502. Cabot, argue the historians who are convinced of his success, should be recognized for being one of the first of the Renaissance explorers to find the New World.

Most scholars, however, work beyond nationalism and pride to understand the facts of the past and its people. To this day, there is still debate about this actual landing site. Was it in the frozen lands of Labrador, part of the province of Newfoundland, or the warmer but rockier shores off the coast of Nova Scotia? Some even argue he didn't land in Canada at all, but rather in coastal Maine. Another question is whether Cabot himself believed that he had found a new land, or, like Columbus, the mainland of Asia.

The answers to many questions about Cabot's life still elude historians. Historical documents and archaeological evidence do not reveal other pertinent information about Cabot's life either, such as exactly when he was born, what he looked like, or how he died.

Scholars are forced to piece facts together about the explorer's history from legal documents and letters that are scattered in the archives of at least three nations—England, Italy, and Spain. They reveal few details about his dealings as a merchant and any business partnerships he had. Historians have learned little about his efforts to gain **patronage** from King Henry VII of England, who officially supported, but did not fund, Cabot's voyage. The king hoped that the Venetian navigator would find new lands to claim for England.

The research continues, particularly in the hunt for a ship's log documenting his journey. So far, no such information has been discovered, but newer documentation uncovered in 2010 has shed some light on one of Cabot's possible patrons. This type of discovery has encouraged historians to continue searching for even more information in order to finally solve the riddle of John Cabot's life.

Chapter 1
The Early Life of Giovanni Caboto

The first man to sail to the New World for England, John Cabot was originally a Venetian citizen. Records confirm that the **city-state**'s senate voted to make him a citizen in 1476. The vote was unanimous.

Historical documents verify that John Cabot was a citizen of Venice, a bustling city located on the northeast coast of the Italian peninsula.

The document recording the vote, written in Latin, tells historians that Cabot was not born in Venice. To become a citizen, he must have lived there for at least fifteen years. Merely having an address in the city, though, did not grant a person citizenship without first proving his honor. In this case, Cabot needed to have shown the people of Venice that he was a responsible member of the community. To some historians, Venice's requirements for citizenship suggested that Cabot must have been an adult when he requested citizenship, perhaps as young as twenty-eight years of age. Other scholars have suggested that he could have been as young as sixteen years old, but historians normally calculate Cabot's age based upon the death date of his son Sebastian Cabot, who died in 1557 as a very old man. This has also helped scholars estimate John Cabot's birth year at about 1450.

Cabot's name next appears in Venetian archives on January 13, 1484, as a married man. The record shows that his wife's family

Fifteenth-century Venice was an important seaport and one of the centers for trade in the Mediterranean.

John Cabot

transferred a **dowry** worth seventy-five ducats to him. In return, he gave a bond, or receipt, to "Mathye [Mattea], my beloved wife." The date of these records, however, does not suggest Cabot's actual wedding date, though historians believe he may have been married in 1474, ten years before the money was transferred, as was the tradition.

WHO IS JOHN CABOT?

Not surprisingly, the man whom history refers to as John Cabot never used the English version of his name. Nor did he use the name dictionaries and encyclopedias refer to as the Italian version of his name, Giovanni Caboto. No original historical documents contain either spelling.

Cabot lived at a time when documents were handwritten and when words, especially names, were spelled in a variety of ways. Some of the many variations of Cabot's name preserved in records written in Latin, Italian, Spanish, and English include Zuan Caboto, Joannes Caboto, Johannes Caboto, and even Zuam Talbot.

By 1496, Cabot had fathered three sons with his wife. Their names were Ludovico, Sebastian, and Sancto. Although little is known of Ludovico and Sancto, Sebastian later became famous himself as an explorer of the New World on behalf of England and Spain.

Historians believe that Cabot was born in **Genoa**, a city-state on the northwestern shore of Italy. His father, Giulio Caboto, was a spice merchant. In the late 1400s, Genoa was an important seaport. Cabot was "another Genoese," like Christopher Columbus, according to Pedro de Ayala, a representative from Spain, in a letter he wrote to King Ferdinand and Queen Isabella of Spain in 1498. Sebastian Cabot also identified his father as a Genoese, though no record of his birth survives there.

Historians believe that, like the lives of other common people, the story of Cabot's birth and youth were not significant enough to have been recorded.

Other Possible Birth Locations

While most historians accept the statements of Pedro de Ayala and Sebastian Cabot, who both claimed that John Cabot's birthplace was Genoa, two alternative possibilities of his origin have yet to be disproved. Records in Valencia, Spain, contain a letter written by King Ferdinand in 1492 that identifies "Johan Caboto Montecalunya, the Venetian." This mariner proposed building a major port on the beach of Valencia, Spain. Historians have not been able to find a meaning for the word "Montecalunya," but some suggest that it has a Spanish origin, particularly a dialect from Catalonia—a region of Spain north of Valencia—which suggests that Cabot may have been born in Spain.

In one other case, the English historian Rawdon Brown wrote on a copy of his 1838 article as it was recounted in the James A. Williamson book, *The Cabot Voyages and Bristol Discovery Under Henry VII*, that he had found new evidence about Cabot's origin. Brown claimed he had found proof that the man who established England's claim to the newly discovered continent was English by birth. Many historians have argued recently that Brown's claim was an attempt at nationalism. They say Brown was trying to support with hindsight England's claim to the land and its riches. The documents to which Brown referred have never been found, despite intense searches.

Working in Venice

Cabot was a Venetian merchant, according to a letter written in December 1497 by Raimondo de Soncino to the duke of

Milan, telling him of Cabot's recent voyage. Apparently, de Soncino knew Cabot well and talked with him about his life. Cabot was an expert mariner and a skilled navigator, according to de Soncino, and would have been well acquainted with the art of sailing the ocean. At the time Cabot learned to sail, he was familiar with the highly lucrative North African spice trade.

De Soncino wrote that Cabot had told him of previous trips to Mecca, an ancient city on the Arabian Peninsula. There Cabot likely learned of the riches traders brought overland by caravan from Eastern countries such as **Cathay** (China) and **Cipango** (Japan). In the markets of Mecca, Cabot would have learned of the months it took men and animals to haul the spices on foot and caravan through the deserts of distant lands. He also probably heard stories of other peoples or great societies. It was in Mecca that Cabot most likely began his dream of finding an ocean route, rather than one over land, to those Asian riches.

This fifteenth-century map of the world illustrates the problems with world trade. European merchants had to travels long distances across dangerous land routes to reach the riches of the Middle East and Asia, because a faster, less expensive water route was not yet known.

A World of Riches

Europeans had been trading with Asian powers for centuries along a route that was commonly known as the Silk Road. Named after the lucrative trade in Chinese silk, the Silk Road introduced many eastern products to Europeans in 330 BC. At this time, Alexander the Great of Macedon conquered huge swaths of the Middle East, colonizing the lands as far east as India. With the establishment of the city Alexandria-Eschate (Alexandria The Furthest), Greek culture and civilization was introduced to the region. The existing trade between China and Middle Eastern countries, such as Persia and Syria, was opened to European markets. Towns sprang up along the route to cater to merchants traveling with the caravans transporting riches back and forth. The route proved so profitable that entire kingdoms taking advantage of the booming trade rose in prominence through the centuries.

European missionaries and traders returning from the Silk Road brought back stories of great wealth in the East. The most well known of these is Marco Polo, a merchant who, like John Cabot, was from Venice. In 1271, when Polo was only seventeen, he traveled East along the Silk Road with his father and uncle. He eventually arrived at Xanadu, in present-day Beijing, China, where he met Kublai Khan, the ruler of the Mongolian Empire. Polo documented these experiences in *The Travels of Marco Polo*, which describes the vast riches and exotic people he encountered during his journey. The book went a long way toward inspiring explorers to search for easy trade routes to Asia, including Christopher Columbus, who is told to have carried a copy of Polo's *Travels* along with him on his voyages to the New World.

By the time Marco Polo had returned to Europe and began telling stories of what he encountered during his travels, the Silk

Road was beginning to crumble. Kublai Khan had died, and without the ruthless central authority of the Mongols to control them, many of the various tribal peoples who lived along the route reclaimed their land. Further complicating matters was the rise of the Islamic Ottoman Empire, which, in 1453, conquered the city of Constantinople in present-day Turkey. Constantinople had once been a major Christian cultural and economic center, and was in large part a gateway to the East. Under control of the Ottoman Empire, the Christian West could no longer access the wealth to the East. The once-prosperous Silk Road had become a long, dangerous journey across wild terrain, making it too expensive for many Europeans in the distant West to travel.

The Need for a Westward Passage

With the Silk Road all but closed, Europeans began searching for alternate routes to the East, particularly sea routes. Since a ship could cover more distance in less time than can a slow land caravan, such a sea route would once again open up Europe to the wealth of the Asia. Excited by the possibility of a cheaper, faster way to Asia, many European nations, including Spain, Portugal, and England, began hiring trained seamen to search for sea routes to Asia. The Renaissance, a period of rebirth for art and learning in Europe, had also reached the heights of artistic and scientific influence in the fifteenth century. This time of intense cultural activity served as a transition period between the Middle Ages, which lasted from the fifth through thirteenth centuries, and the more modern, scientific era. Navigation, exploration, and expanding European trade routes were other primary characteristics of this dynamic period. Between the advances in science, particularly in navigation, and the thirst for cheaper trade with Asia, Europe was on the verge of the great

Age of Discovery. Cabot, along with other explorers of the day, was a part of that intense journey of expansion and discovery.

Cabot probably spoke with friends about locating Cipango, the ancient land of the Far East made famous by Marco Polo. Cabot longed to reach Asia and its wondrous riches, and his trade missions to Mecca ignited and fed his dream.

Unlike many of his contemporaries, who explored easterly trade routes to Asia along the tip of South Africa, Cabot had other ideas. Although such an easterly route was indeed faster than the alternative land route, it still involved months of difficult sailing and included long stretches of difficult sailing. Cabot supposed that if caravans carried riches for months and years across the great land mass of Asia, then ships sailing westward around Earth could reach those same lands of wealth in much less time. Cabot's dream was based on the resurgence of knowledge in Europe from ancient **cartographers** such as Claudius Ptolemy, who estimated the size of Earth when he created the first map of the world in his groundbreaking book, *Geography*. While most people at the time understood that Earth was round, navigators also underestimated its total size. Cabot, like his contemporary Columbus, did not believe the world was large enough to hold two additional continents and two vast oceans.

Another letter offers evidence of Cabot's desire to sail west to Asia. In 1498, the same year that Vasco da Gama navigated a sea route to India for Portugal, de Ayala, in a letter to the Spanish **monarchs**, confirmed that Cabot had been to Lisbon, Portugal, and Seville, Spain, "seeking persons to aid him in [his] discovery [of foreign trade routes]."

These discussions are the only evidence of Cabot's early career as a navigator, yet historians argue that only the merchants of

Italian port cities such as Venice or Genoa, and not Bristol, England, could have had enough knowledge of navigation to attempt a voyage across the Atlantic in the 1400s. Historians suggest that King Henry VII hired Cabot because of his specific abilities as a navigator, valuable skills that he most likely would have gained only in Italy.

In order for the king of England to give Cabot a charter to sail on behalf of the country, Henry VII would had to have known that Cabot was capable of such a difficult journey. The fact that Cabot was able to secure investors in England—and as it's now known, Italy as well—demonstrated that he was able to convince the right people of his skills and abilities as a sailor and navigator. Certainly, Cabot's desire to reach Japan by sailing west from Europe was something the king and the merchants wanted. That way, they could reap the rich rewards that would arise from the new trade route.

Cartographers at the time of Cabot had made fairly accurate maps of known locations, such as the Mediterranean shown here, but could not imagine the existence of two continents and an ocean in addition.

Chapter 2
Exploring the North Atlantic

For years, historians claimed that John Cabot was the first European to reach the present-day country of Canada. However, researchers now know that the Norsemen of Scandinavia, commonly known as Vikings, reached Canada almost 500 years earlier.

Although explorers such as Columbus and Cabot are commonly credited with "discovering" America, Norse Vikings had actually made settlements on North America nearly 500 years earlier.

In addition, European fishermen also sailed in the region. However, Cabot was the first to make a formal claim on the land for another country.

Cabot's command of the *Matthew* in 1497 marked an end to the haphazard and chance landings on the North American continent. It led to the beginning of well-informed, planned, and successful expeditions and explorations for the kingdom of England.

EARLY EUROPEANS IN AMERICA

The evidence of Norse visits to the shores of North America stems from archaeological research conducted in Greenland and from legends and documents that have survived in Iceland and Norway. Erik Thorvaldsson, known as Erik the Red, after being exiled from his native Norway and then from Iceland, traveled in 985 CE with fourteen ships filled with family members and colonists to settle in western Greenland.

Research by archaeologist Kirsten Seaver suggests that Erik and his companions frequently traveled to the coast of Labrador, a province of Newfoundland, Canada, which lies more than 500 miles west of Greenland. Other studies indicate that Norse sailors may have traveled as far south as Nova Scotia and the Saint Lawrence River. Further research, primarily by Canadian archaeologists, shows that Erik the Red's son established a permanent Norse presence in what is now L'Anse aux Meadows on the northern part of the island of Newfoundland.

A closer examination of Scandinavian documents also suggests that for centuries Norse settlers in Greenland made seasonal journeys along the North American coast, harvesting foods from its ocean and shore. Historians think that the Norse descendants inhabited Greenland in the early 1400s and may have been visited frequently by fishermen from Iceland, Ireland, and England.

The port city of Bristol, located in southeast England, was a center for maritime trade and fishing. It is suspected that Bristol fisherman at the time of Cabot's voyage had knowledge of the distant coasts of North America.

Bristol Sailors in North America

Research into the merchant trade of England has led to a significant understanding of the trading business that built the English port city of Bristol. For example, in 1956 a letter was discovered in the Spanish archives in **Simancas**, Spain. It was written by Bristol merchant John Day late in 1497, and told of ocean voyages in the 1480s. "It is considered certain that the cape of the said land [upon which Cabot landed on June 24, 1497] was found and discovered in the past by the men from Bristol." This statement, by a man who had firsthand knowledge of Bristol's business, suggested that merchants had financed annual expeditions of fishing fleets to the unnamed land across the Atlantic Ocean since late in the fifteenth century. Additional evidence suggests that the Bristol merchants, as long as they could have afforded to, also had sent expeditions to the west.

Historians and archaeologists have worked to uncover evidence of any connection between Europe and North America. In many instances, they have provided evidence of almost continuous seafaring between the two continents. Scholars have gathered so much evidence, in fact, that many have developed theories about how Cabot, a navigator who knew well the waters of the Mediterranean Sea and the Atlantic Ocean along Europe's western shores, "discovered" a new continent.

The trouble with their theories is that North America was not lost. Scholars increasingly point out that some Europeans already knew that the land existed. And although mariners did not know the extent of the continent, they apparently believed that the distant shore was not Asia. This was contrary to the beliefs of many more experienced navigators.

Reaching Asia by Sailing West

For Cabot, the late fifteenth century marked a perfect moment to combine his personal business interests with the political and expansionary goals of England's king, Henry VII. As historical documents suggested, Henry wanted to control those same riches and, in the event that a continent stood between England and Asia, to gain **dominion** over whatever lands could officially be made known to him.

In the patent letters (public letters) of March 5, 1496, Henry VII gave "full and free authority, faculty, and power to sail to all parts, regions, and coasts of the eastern, western, and northern sea, under [England's] banners, flags, and ensigns." This authority from England's king made Cabot's voyage of exploration more important than any of its prior voyages.

Once news of Columbus' successful journey across the Atlantic Ocean on behalf of the Spanish crown reached the

Motivated by reports of Columbus's discoveries on behalf of the Spanish crown, King Henry VII sought to claim the New World on behalf of England.

rest of Europe, other nations wanted in on this "New World." Finding seasoned sailors capable of making the dangerous journey across the ocean to explore the new continents, as well as continue to search for a passage to Asia, was the goal of several European nations. Despite not having a significant navy, England was still interested in staking claim to these new lands, and Cabot was a natural choice for their expeditions.

Chapter 3

Relocating to England

J ohn Cabot's abilities as a sailor and navigator were no doubt sharpened by repeated voyages around the Mediterranean Sea, sailing in and out of the ports in Spain, Italy, and the Middle East. This led Raimondo di Soncino to describe Cabot as "a most expert mariner,"

John Cabot may have been among the crowd when Christopher Columbus and his ships returned from the New World.

one whose experience would allow him to sail across the Atlantic Ocean. However, there is little to no recorded information about Cabot's sailing career before he headed across the Atlantic, so historians need to speculate about his experience based on the behavior of other seamen from the same era.

As a young man, Cabot likely served in many positions aboard ship, apprenticing to captains, studying nautical instruments, and learning about life at sea. A trip from Venice to Mecca on the Arabian Peninsula, for instance, would have involved crossing the Mediterranean Sea to Alexandria, Egypt, and then setting out across land in a southward direction. If he was the same Johan Caboto Montecalunya who in 1492 proposed building a port in Valencia, then he would have learned about harbors, the depth of water needed to bring in trading vessels of the era, and the materials needed to establish a stable ocean floor.

Inspired by Columbus

While Cabot's journey to Mecca had taught him about the spices, gems, clothes, and woods that came in abundance from Asia, he shared Columbus's dream of finding a sea route to its shores. He also believed that traveling in the opposite direction, sailing west, would bring him more swiftly to those riches.

In March 1493, when Columbus was welcomed to the harbor at Palos, Spain, from his first journey across the Atlantic Ocean, Cabot may have been there. If Johan Caboto Montecalunya is the same Cabot who sailed to the new lands in 1497, then he was in Valencia, on the Mediterranean coast, when Columbus returned. Cabot could have been among the crowds that welcomed the Genoese hero in cities across Spain. It is possible that Cabot met Columbus and doubted his story about reaching Asian shores.

The Science of Sailing

If Cabot was born in 1450, he would have been forty-six years of age when King Henry VII approved his Atlantic Ocean crossing. By 1496, Cabot could easily have gained more than thirty years of experience at sea. He would have been well acquainted with the astrolabe and the cross-staff, and perhaps even the quadrant, all devices for determining latitude, or positions north

A nautical astrolabe, much like the one Cabot would have used.

and south. He would have known how to use a magnetic compass for finding direction. Yet Cabot, like his colleagues, would have had great difficulty measuring longitude, or positions east and west, for that skill eluded navigators until the development of reliable marine clocks in the 1700s.

Most scholars suggest that knowledge of Earth's spherical shape was understood among the people of Europe in the 1400s. While that view was shared by the masses, many historians also believe that the educated elite had for centuries thought that the world was round. Columbus, Vespucci, Magellan, and other European explorers had the scientific knowledge and the skills to understand that Earth is round.

These same navigators, however, lacked a true understanding of Earth's size, or circumference. Cabot, like his peers, believed that a short journey of one to two months lay ahead of them when they set sail in a westerly direction to Asia. They did not understand or appreciate that the world was large enough to contain two additional continents and two huge oceans. Europeans did not realize until the early sixteenth century that the great Eastern Ocean, about which Marco Polo had written of in his memoirs (1298), was not the same ocean that lapped upon the shores of Europe.

Once he had heard of Columbus's failure to reach Asia in warmer waters, Cabot, some historians argue, probably concluded that a journey across the Atlantic Ocean's cold northern latitudes would be more effective. Because Earth's lines of longitude are much closer together in the north because of the curvature of the planet, he concluded, the journey would be swifter. Cabot believed he could sail westward in far fewer days than the ten weeks Columbus had required. He may have thought he could reach the Asian mainland in record time before sailing in a southerly direction along the coast until he found the great societies of Marco Polo's stories.

Even if Montecalunya is not the same man who made that North Atlantic journey, historians suggest that England's Cabot would have also been well acquainted with Columbus's struggle in the 1480s to find a government to support his quest.

Although reports of Christopher Columbus's voyage were shocking to Europeans, he did not, as he intended, find a westward route to Asia.

Cabot, a Genoese navigator like Columbus, could easily have learned of any efforts to cross the Atlantic in the southern latitudes. Cabot, sharing that dream, could have formed his own plan, influenced by Columbus's reasoning, to reach the same destination by a shorter, northern route.

Cabot apparently also sought financial support from the leaders of Spain and Portugal, just as Columbus did. Cabot, however, found little success in those countries. Spain had already agreed to pay for Columbus's journeys, supporting a second voyage of seventeen ships and 1,500 men that would not return until 1496. Portugal had little interest in repeating Spain's success and instead pursued its own goal of exploring the western coast of Africa. Portugal had a critical success when Vasco da Gama, a Portuguese navigator, became the first European explorer to round the Cape of Good Hope on his journey to India from 1497 to 1498. That said, England remained the next best seafaring kingdom after Portugal and Spain that Cabot could approach with his dream of westward exploration.

Bustling Bristol

The ports of Europe in the 1400s were busy places, with people from around the known world meeting, talking, and sharing information. Bristol merchants traveled to Portugal, Spain, and Italy, just as merchants from Venice traveled to Spain, Portugal, and England. Historical records of the day-to-day activities of trading centers that lined the Mediterranean Sea and Europe's coast suggest that Cabot most likely met merchants from many distant cities, including Bristol, as he traveled to find financial support for his voyage.

It is also possible that merchants from Bristol traveled to foreign ports seeking a talented navigator willing to take on such an adventure on England's behalf. Or Cabot easily could have made contact with such merchants in Venice, Seville, or Lisbon and reached a business agreement that took him to the royal court of England.

Cabot most likely moved with his family to England in the mid-1490s, a time when he, a talented Venetian merchant, might have seen opportunities for exploration. By helping England achieve its mercantile goals and enabling its king to enter the competition to reach Asia by sea, Cabot could also fulfill his own ambitions.

By 1495, Cabot, his wife, and their three sons had become residents of Bristol, where they rented a small house on Saint Nicholas Street. Bristol was a lively, thriving city of cobblestone streets and row houses located at the junction of the River Avon and the River Frome, just about eight miles from where the Avon empties into the Bristol Channel. The Avon was a treacherous waterway: Not only was it difficult to navigate, but also its tidal flow was extremely forceful. Still, Bristol's location was in a prime position if one were thinking of sailing toward the channel and farther into the Atlantic Ocean in a westerly direction, as Cabot had intended.

Once there, Cabot met merchants who would later help him finance his voyage. He became friendly with two of Bristol's most successful businessmen, Robert Thorne and Hugh Elyot. Both men provided details about the city's trading history, its interests, and recent voyages. In turn, Cabot certainly shared his desires of searching for unknown lands in the name of England.

By the end of the fifteenth century, Bristol—then a city of 10,000 people—had become England's most prosperous port, importing and exporting taxable goods such as cloth, wine, and dyes to and from Spain, Portugal, and Ireland, and wool and salt to Iceland. However, trade in Iceland had slowed, and its fishing industry was facing an economic slump. English sailors had conflicting trade agreements with Icelanders for years, the results of which were finally beginning to affect profits. Because of this, England was in search of a new base for lucrative fishing operations that would result in increased profits. To solve this problem, Bristol had seen many ships leave its docks in search of new lands and untouched fishing grounds.

The Mythical Island of Brasil

Around the time John Cabot first sailed for North America, Europeans still had an incomplete understanding of the world. The science of navigation was still being developed, and many maps were made using the rough measurements and estimates of navigators using primitive tools. This meant that even the most detailed maps were often inaccurate. The shapes of continents and coastlines were distorted and looked nothing like the actual shapes of continents we know today. No matter how good the map, though, whole sections of the globe were still undiscovered. As a result, these unexplored waters were filled by the imaginations of sailors and sea captains, who made up stories about exotic lands filled with riches and seaways populated by huge monsters.

The mariners and ship captains who worked the port in Bristol were no exception. They believed in the existence of distant, but unknown, lands in the Atlantic Ocean. Sailors, who often spoke about what they had heard or seen on their voyages, shared stories about an island called **Brasil** (also known as Hy-Brasil) that was said to lie off the western coast of Ireland. Other legends claimed that there was another island, too, only this one contained fabulous riches and was known as the "Island of the Seven Cities."

Brasil (top left), off the west coast of Ireland (center), was just one example of a hypothetical land that Europeans had not yet explored. Although Brasil turned out to be a myth, Cabot used such theories to convince the English king to support his voyage.

English ships had been searching for undiscovered territory in the Atlantic since 1480. Some historians believe that British sailors explored areas as far north as present-day Canada. A few sailors claimed they had spotted the sight of land to the south and west of Greenland in waters that were regularly traveled by English boats.

This news excited Cabot, who knew he could use the evidence of distant, unknown lands to convince King Henry VII to support an official voyage of exploration. To Cabot, these islands of riches sounded like the islands lying off the coast of Asia—the same islands that Columbus mistakenly believed he had found in 1492.

To make his journey possible, Cabot needed merchants, banks, and the crown to provide financial and political backing. In addition to meeting with King Henry VII, Cabot also traveled throughout Bristol looking for patrons to bankroll his voyage west in his search for Asia.

Chapter 4

First to the New World

As an able sailor, navigator, and cartographer, Cabot traveled to Bristol, England, in order to fund his dream to travel the high seas, in search of new lands to discover, chart, and claim for England.

Inspired by Marco Polo, John Cabot would secure the support needed to explore the wider world.

Cabot's hope was to sail to Asia, not around the long, unknown coast of Africa, but by the shorter route, a westward journey across the Atlantic Ocean. He and other Italian mariners of the day, most notably Columbus, believed a direct route lay to the west of Europe. If the world was round, they reasoned, the journey was possible.

Fueled by the stories he heard in England, his experiences while trading in the Middle East and Egypt, and his interest in Marco Polo, who had told the world of the great riches of Asia 200 years earlier, Cabot was about to fulfill his destiny.

DIVIDING THE NEW WORLD

King Henry VII supported Cabot's decision to sail west in search of a new sea route to Asia's wealth. By doing so, though, he risked the possibility of conflict with Portugal and Spain, since both kingdoms had staked claims to lands in the Atlantic Ocean. Together, both had signed the Treaty of Tordesillas in 1494, which divided the lands in the Atlantic Ocean by an imaginary line.

The terms of this treaty, which divided the area vertically from the North Pole to the South Pole 370 **leagues** (approximately 1,100 miles) west of the Cape Verde Islands, gave Spain all lands west of the line and Portugal all lands east of it. Since Henry VII had not been invited to sign the treaty, he did not recognize this division. Therefore,

In exploring North America, King Henry VII risked angering Spain and Portugal, who had signed a treaty dividing all new lands between them along the line mapped above.

he decided that undiscovered lands in the same latitude as England were available for exploration by any navigator sailing under the English flag.

An Audience with the King

Historians argue over his method, but somehow Cabot convinced King Henry VII to give public support to his expedition. Cabot traveled to London and the king's court in late 1495 or early 1496 to begin to plead his case with his advisers and then, eventually, with the king himself.

Originally, history provided no evidence of how Henry VII came to sign the charter, or **patent letters,** for Cabot's voyage. Recent research suggests that Cabot was introduced to the king by a papal diplomat named Giovanni Antonio de Carbonariis, who clearly thought enough of his fellow Italian *émigré* to recommend his abilities to the king. Through his own words or words drafted for him, Henry granted to the "well-beloved John Cabot, citizen of Venice" permission to sail west from England's shores, "under [England's] banners flags and ensigns," seeking "islands, countries, regions or provinces . . . which before this time were unknown to all Christians."

Scholars of the late twentieth and early twenty-first centuries suggest that Cabot became a public symbol for Henry VII's efforts to expand England's kingdom. Now that Spain was gaining a foothold on the lands of the New World, England, then a country of great poverty, was pressured to discover new lands and trade routes of its own. The Black Plague and a long civil war had left the kingdom politically divided and virtually bankrupt. If Cabot was correct in his belief about the mysterious islands lying off the coast of Asia, England could then single-handedly control the elusive and profitable spice trade, saving the country from financial ruin. Surely, Cabot probably argued, the English could still beat the Portuguese and Spaniards to China and Japan, especially since by his reasoning Asia was physically closer to England than either of those kingdoms.

The king, having refused official support to Columbus years earlier, did not wish to make a similar mistake this time. In this very knowledgeable Venetian merchant, Henry VII likely saw the opportunity to successfully enter a kingdom-building venture.

Preparing to Make Way

Cabot finally received the king's permission to sail on March 5, 1496. His plan for reaching Asia was to exploit Bristol's strongest winds while sailing down the Avon to the mouth of the Bristol Channel and into the sea. Next, he planned to travel across a short section of the Atlantic Ocean to southern Ireland before heading west from the shores north of Dursey Head.

While Cabot had gained his experience sailing around the Mediterranean Sea, Bristol's merchants knew very well the fishing waters off the coast of Iceland, more than 800 miles (1,287 kilometers) north-northwest of their English port. They also understood the seasonal winds of the waters around England. Cabot, applying his expertise to this knowledge, was determined to catch the easterly winds of late May to power his journey. For some reason, however, Cabot's memorable voyage of 1497 set out fourteen months after the king had authorized it.

Initial Failure

For the first 450 years after John Cabot was known to have reached the North American continent, historians, some who lived during Cabot's lifetime, recorded only the story of his 1497 voyage. However, in 1956, a scholar named L. A. Vigneras, studying in Spain's national archives in Simancas, uncovered evidence that Cabot actually did set sail in a westward direction as soon as possible after receiving the king's permission.

Vigneras uncovered a letter among centuries-old records, written by English merchant John Day to the *almirante* mayor (grand admiral) of Castile, Spain. In the letter, Day provides details relating to Cabot's first failed attempt to cross the Atlantic Ocean. "He [Cabot] went with one ship, his crew confused him, he was short of supplies and ran into bad weather and he decided to turn back," the letter read, according to James A. Williamson's book, *The Cabot Voyages*. Since the discovery of that letter, historians have concluded that Day was writing to Columbus.

Historians have long puzzled over Cabot's reason for waiting more than a year to set sail from England. Day's letter reveals that Cabot took advantage of the king's support immediately. That failed effort may have been the result of a distrustful crew who feared the cold ocean waters. Perhaps doubting his acclaimed expertise, Cabot's men may have been frightened by dangerous ocean storms and revolted against their captain. They likely refused to take the ship in the direction Cabot commanded. With no other choice, the explorer returned to Bristol to wait for better weather conditions and more supplies.

Further Planning

No one knows about the specific plans Cabot made for his voyages. The charter of 1496 from King Henry VII granted the explorer permission to take "five ships or vessels of whatsoever burden and quality they may be, and with so many and with such mariners and men as they may wish to take with them," according to Williamson in *The Cabot Voyages*. In that same letter, however, the king promised no money from the royal **exchequer** (England's department of revenue). He placed all of the responsibility for financing the ship on Cabot, who sought the aid of area merchants.

For centuries, it was assumed that Cabot's only support came from British interests. However, in 2010 documentation proved that the Bardi firm, an Italian bank at the time, also contributed to the finances of the voyage. During the Age of Discovery, Bardi had supported other explorers, including Christopher Columbus and Amerigo Vespucci. Historians theorize that the Bardi firm gave money to Cabot in order to stay in the good graces of the papal emissary who had endorsed him: Carbonariis.

If Cabot planned his voyage as a hired expert for Bristol's merchants in order to locate the lost island of Brasil, then as the poor man he was known to be, Cabot must have relied on other benefactors to pay for his journey.

Although Henry VII had approved sending five ships in his name, only one small ship set sail from Bristol in May 1497. A *navicula* (little ship) capable of carrying a mere fifty tons of wine and needing a crew of no more than twenty to maneuver and maintain her, was all Cabot had at his disposal for this journey.

Setting Sail

Cabot set sail from Bristol, England, in late May 1497, most likely on May 22. He would have sailed early in the morning to catch the outgoing tides that carried his ship down the River Avon and into the Bristol Channel.

Cabot set forth aboard the *Matthew* (also spelled *Mathew*, a ship certainly named after Cabot's wife, Mattea), a small, three-masted vessel, with a crew of eighteen to twenty men. He was likely excited and nervous at the adventure ahead, knowing that the ocean winds could propel him westward or force him once again back to England.

The most detailed account of Cabot's voyage survives in a letter written by John Day, the same sailor who wrote to Columbus about Cabot's first failed voyage. Day wrote to an Italian explorer who had also made two crossings of the Atlantic. His experience enabled him to include nautical facts that have given historians detailed accounts of Cabot's journey, based on conversations with the explorer himself.

From the Bristol Channel, Cabot set his course for Dursey Head, Ireland, a promontory, or highest point, of the island's southwestern tip. Once there, Cabot dropped anchor and made evening sightings of the North Star before the main journey began. Cabot intended to follow the line of latitude that crosses Dursey Head in a northerly direction. With his bearings taken, he commanded his crew to weigh anchor, and his journey into unknown waters began.

His voyage took up to thirty-three days, according to Day. An east-northeast wind and calm seas made for a fast journey. It is likely, however, that Cabot spent some of this time struggling against variable winds and skirting ice floes still floating in the cold spring waters.

Rear admiral and historian, Samuel Eliot Morison (1887–1976), who served in the U.S. Naval Reserve during World War II, captured the sense of Cabot's voyage in his book, *The European Discovery of North America*. In his research, Morison crossed the Atlantic Ocean along Cabot's route and studied the documents and maps of the fifteenth and sixteen centuries. Morison's image of Cabot shows a man tacking (adjusting the sails to change direction) across winds that did not blow due east. Cabot likely would have needed to sail around icebergs in western waters. Fog often shrouds the coast north of central Nova Scotia (45 degrees latitude), and Cabot would have needed to use his navigational skills to find his way through that fog.

Near the journey's end, Cabot would have sensed land looming ahead. He would have seen low-lying clouds and pieces of trees and plants drifting on the water, and even smelled the aromas of fir trees as they wafted out from the shore. At that, he would have begun taking soundings, which involves dropping the lead weight into the sea to check its depth. He also would have brought up samples from the ocean floor. At five o'clock one June morning, according to a map drawn years later by Cabot's son

Where Cabot Landed

No one knows exactly where John Cabot landed on June 24, 1497. Since the late 1700s, historians have speculated that Cabot set foot as far north as Baffin Island or as far south as Cape Cod, Massachusetts. Below are some of the most widely believed locations of Cabot's official landing site, listed from north to south:

In Canada:

    Baffin Island

    Cape Chidley, northern tip of Labrador

    Near Domino, south of Sandwich Bay, Labrador

    Cape St. Lewis, near Fox Harbour, Labrador

    Cape Bonavista, Newfoundland

    Cape Dégrat, Newfoundland

    Cape Race, Newfoundland

    Cape Bauld, Newfoundland, in the Strait of Belle Isle

    Cape North, island of Cape Breton, Nova Scotia

    Cape Sable, southwest Nova Scotia

In the United States:

    Maine

    Cape Cod, Massachusetts

Sebastian, a rugged shore rose before the *Matthew*, as a breeze dispersed the early morning fog.

On June 24, 1497, Cabot, with a small crew of sailors from southern England, set foot upon the shores of North America and officially claimed its land for England.

The New Found Land

That long day became memorable for Cabot and his son Sebastian, who recalled it almost fifty years later. It also marked the date of the feast of St. John the Baptist, the day that celebrates the birth of this New Testament prophet.

The location of Cabot's landfall, however, remains puzzling. The shore, after all, was unknown to all who sailed on the *Matthew*. With no surviving ship logs to record Cabot's navigational readings from his cross-staff, astrolabe, or compass, historians find themselves having to piece together bits of information from letters and copies of maps drawn in the 1500s.

Morison believed that Cabot landed in Griquet Harbor,

Cabot's actual landing spot is still debated. There is evidence that supports a variety of locations along the coast of northeast Canada and the United States.

4 miles (6 km) south of Cape Dégrat, which on modern maps would be on the top of Cape Bauld on the northern-most shore of Newfoundland. Other historians are less certain.

During the 1800s and 1900s, scholars argued that Cabot's landfall might have taken place as far north as Baffin Island in Canada, or as far south as Cape Cod, Massachusetts.

Cabot and his crew went ashore the morning of first sighting and raised several flags, most likely the coat of arms of King Henry VII. Some sources mention the flag of St. Mark, the emblem of Venice. Others think Cabot raised either a crucifix or a flag to honor Pope Alexander VI, the leader of the Roman Catholic Church from 1491 to 1503.

Once onshore, Cabot and his crew "found tall trees of the kind masts are made, and other smaller trees," Day said in his letters as told in Williamson's *The Cabot Voyages*. They also found a trail that led inland, a site where a campfire had once burned, and a stick some 18 inches (46 centimeters) long that had been pierced at both ends, carved, and painted red. Cabot also reported finding snares for capturing animals and needles for making nets, all signs that the lands were inhabited.

The brief exploration of land on that June morning was the only time Cabot or his crew set foot on this "new found land." Not sure of the reception they would receive from the inhabitants, and being on one defenseless ship with a small crew, Cabot chose to be careful. Cabot would have good reason to be cautious. He knew from his travels to the Middle East, if he was indeed in Asia, that the land would be well inhabited. He would not have wanted to risk the lives of his crew and fail to return to England with news of his discovery.

After leaving that landfall, Cabot guided the *Matthew* along the coast of eastern Canada, exploring the bays and inlets, mapping his findings, and searching for any signs of inhabitants. The forest was dense and beautiful, and there were what appeared to be small villages dotting the shoreline. The crew found an abundance of fish, as Williamson reported in *The Cabot Voyages*, "like those in Iceland [that] are dried in the open and sold in England and other countries," and that are sometimes called stockfish in England. Cabot and his crew also saw the shadows of two forms running after one another on land but could not determine whether they were human beings or animals.

Many archaeologists and historians suggest that those stockfish, also known as cod, were England's primary reason for seeking out new lands to explore. Fifteenth-century fisheries of Western Europe, particularly those near Iceland, had been badly depleted of this main source of food.

Difficult Sailing

The few surviving documents that describe Cabot's journey cannot capture the challenge or the danger of that Canadian coastline, according to Morison. These were new waters for Cabot, who was a very intelligent man and experienced navigator. An expert mariner, Morison argued, would have known the dangers of facing unknown waters and shores.

The coast Cabot sailed is as rugged a shoreline today as it was in the late 1400s. Treacherous rocks hide below murky waters, while icebergs, even in the summer, cause hazards for sailors of the largest ships. Fog rolls offshore unexpectedly and hides the shoreline even at close distances. Thirty days may sound like a short trip, considering the mission to discover a new land and perhaps encounter people. Yet Cabot's primary goal was to return to England with maps of his journey to help himself and sailors like him repeat the trip. He would not have risked his ship or his crew, historians argue, in any more exploration than they would have needed to establish their "discovery" and document it for their English sponsors.

Returning to England

In his letters, Day suggested that Cabot returned to his original landing site before setting his return course. The highly experienced mariner wanted to follow the same path home that he had taken on the outward crossing. "They returned to the coast of Europe in fifteen days," Day wrote.

The trouble Cabot experienced on the return voyage did not come from the weather or the ocean, but from his crew. The sailors he had hired in Bristol lacked confidence in his navigational instruments and in his skills. After all, Cabot was using instruments well known in port cities such as Venice, Genoa, and Portugal, but little used in England. Day also wrote, "They had the wind behind them, and he reached Brittany because the sailors confused him saying that he was heading too far north." The Bristol merchant sailors had hired an expert, but did not trust his expertise. Still, it was common for the opinions of the ship's crew to have influence on its course.

Because they did not agree with Cabot's decisions, the crew unfortunately took the *Matthew* off its original course, but Cabot was able to use his experience as a navigator to get them back on track. Instead of reaching England, Cabot realized they were farther south, near Brittany and the northeast coast of France. Cabot was able to direct the ship back on course for Bristol, and the ship arrived in early August 1497.

Chapter 5
The Last Voyage

C abot and his crew were back in England in 1497, and were able to tell the English people about the land they had discovered and claimed for the crown during their journey across the Atlantic. Soon after returning to Bristol, Cabot

Cabot's return to England aboard the *Matthew* was met with excitement. From the port of Bristol, Cabot raced to London to meet with King Henry VII and report his discovery.

took another journey—this one by land in a coach across the country in order to have an audience with King Henry VII in his London palace. With the race on among the nations of Europe to claim new lands in both the New World and Asia, the king wanted to hear Cabot's report as quickly as possible. Any land Cabot had claimed in England's name would be the first in the New World for the country.

Records kept of the king's schedule suggest that Henry VII listened to Cabot's report and granted him an immediate gift of ten pounds, a generous sum, as well as an annual pension of twenty pounds.

Cabot's crew had confirmed and supported their commander's story, a fact that made it more believable. In fact, without his English crew to corroborate his findings, Cabot would have had far greater trouble convincing the king that what he said was truthful, according to information attributed to de Soncino in Williamson's *The Cabot Voyages*: "This Messer Zoane [Cabot] as a foreigner and a poor man, would not have obtained credence, had it not been that his companions, who are practically all English and from Bristol, testified that he spoke the truth."

Cabot apparently shared news of the distant land with his many friends, colleagues, and countrymen. Williamson also tells of Cabot's peers who spoke of his now-famous voyage. Lorenzo Pasqualigo, another merchant, wrote on August 23, 1497, "That Venetian of ours who went with a small ship from Bristol to find new islands has come back and says he has discovered mainland 700 leagues away, which is the country of the Grand Khan."

Moreover, Cabot spoke at length with de Soncino, who retold the tale of his voyage to the duke of Milan in a letter written on December 18, 1497. "He [Cabot] tells this in such a way, and makes everything so plain, that I also feel compelled to believe him. What is much more, his Majesty [Henry VII], who is wise and not prodigal, also gives him some credence."

Details of Cabot's voyage remain vague. No journal that Cabot might have written has survived, if, indeed, any actually existed. A captain's log, in which a ship's captain would document events that took place during its voyage, was not yet a part of navigational tradition, and it is possible that Cabot did not keep a personal diary of his journey. However, Renaissance merchants were known to keep nautical charts of their voyages, information they often saved. In this way, as they traveled the coasts of Europe and Africa they could record latitude, compass settings,

CABOT'S LOST MAP AND GLOBE

In addition to the testimony of his crewmembers, Cabot created both a flat map and a globe of his voyage in order to further convince his backers to finance another journey to North America. De Ayala, the junior Spanish ambassador to England, mentioned the map in a letter dated July 25, 1498: "I have seen the map made by the discoverer, who is another Genoese like Columbus." Although certainly loosely drawn, both the map and globe of the new lands Cabot encountered would have added valuable pieces to the puzzle of the wider world. Unfortunately, the map and globe are lost to history.

If Cabot left these items in the care of his partners, as some historians have suggested, those partners lost track of them centuries ago. Historical cartographers greatly regret that his illustrations of the journey did not survive. If they had, Cabot's landfall might be as well known as that of Columbus's. As it is, maps of uncertain quality, copied by people who did not themselves make the journeys they represented, are all that remain to testify to Cabot's voyages. To make matters worse, those maps typically contain confusing dates, latitudes, directions, and perspectives, making them unreliable sources.

and conditions of the ocean's bottom to aid their recollection or to compare to what other sailors had before told them. Still, if Cabot kept such charts, they have yet to be located.

From poorly copied maps and secondhand written accounts, cartographers have tried to identify the lands Cabot explored. With little more than a general sense of his approximate positions, however, determining the exact route of his voyage has been impossible.

Returning to the New World

Enthusiasm for Cabot's official discovery of lands across the Atlantic Ocean was so great that Henry VII, the merchants of Bristol, and Cabot himself began planning a larger expedition for the summer of 1498. Dreams of wealth and fame filled their imaginations.

In August 1497, Lorenzo Pasqualigo wrote, "The king has promised him for the spring ten armed ships as he desires and has given him all the prisoners to be sent away, that they may go with him, as he has requested." It was not unusual for criminals to be assigned duties aboard voyages of discovery and exploration, especially because their lives were not as valued as those of typical citizens. In fact, Columbus's crew on his first voyage to the New World was primarily composed of men who were convicted of one crime or another. They sailed with the then-unknown navigator in exchange for their freedom.

The official records of Milan also contain a summary of news received by the duke in letters that arrived the morning of August 24, 1497. The documents briefly reported Cabot's safe return from his journey across the Atlantic Ocean. In the height of excitement over Cabot's news, they also reported, "This next spring his Majesty means to send him with fifteen or twenty ships."

In December 1497, in a lengthy letter to the duke of Milan, de Soncino wrote this about Cabot's plans for 1498: "Messer Zoane . . . proposes to keep along the coast from the place at which he touched, more and more towards the east, until he reaches an island which he calls Cipango, situated in the equinoctial [equator] region, where he believes that all the spices of the world have their origin as well as the jewels."

Day, the Bristol merchant, wrote to his correspondent in late 1497, "With God's help it is hoped to push through plans for exploring the said land more thoroughly next year with ten or twelve vessels," as told in Williamson's *The Cabot Voyages*.

The months that followed Cabot's return to England were indeed lavish. He is said to have become rather boastful of his accomplishments, parading around the city of Bristol and making promises of riches and land to all of his new friends. These were the promises of a returning hero, John Cabot, a man who quickly became famous in the streets of London. Crowds followed Cabot. People sought him out, paid attention to his speeches, called him "Admiral," and admired the silks he now wore—signs of the king's favors. His crew acted like noble counts led by Cabot, their glorified prince.

Those were the hopes of a man with proof that his dream had come true—one who believed, like Columbus had, that he had actually found a sea route to the riches of Asia. While Columbus struggled among his islands, Cabot thought he had found the Asian mainland.

On his second journey westward, Cabot was to command more than a dozen ships, fitted with a crew of hundreds, not merely a single ship with a crew of eighteen. On them he would carry enough supplies for more than a year of exploration. On this voyage, he and his crew would be prepared to establish an English colony on the claimed shores. They would build a fortress and from there explore the coastline, braving any possible dangers.

After his tremendous and profitable meeting with the king, with promises of a great expedition to plan, Cabot returned to his wife and sons at their rented home in Bristol, near one of the city's main docks. It was there that Cabot made plans for his second expedition.

Financial Setbacks for the Next Journey

By early 1498, Cabot's great dreams were scaled back when the support for his second voyage was decreased. The king, having fought wars against rebels in his own country, did not have the money to spend on risky ocean ventures. On February 3, 1498, Henry VII issued his second patent letter to Cabot. It described plans for a much smaller second voyage than Cabot had hoped to lead: "By thies [this] presentes [presents] geve [give] and graunte [grant] to our wel beloved John Kaboto [Cabot], Venician, sufficient auctorite [authority] and power that he . . . may take at his pleasure vi [six] englisshe shippes . . . and theym convey and lede [lead] to the londe [land] and Iles [islands] of late founde by the seid [said] John in our name."

Expense accounts from the king's official records show that, although he granted permission for six ships to sail, he would finance only one vessel. The king's decision is seen by some historians as stingy in comparison to investments made by other monarchs. The Spanish monarchs, King Ferdinand and Queen Isabella, made generous contributions to finance Columbus's journeys. Support given by the Portuguese monarchs John II (1481–1495) and Manuel I (1495–1521) to find a route around the southern tip of Africa, known today as the Cape of Good Hope, was extensive. One explanation is that England's king was indeed a frugal man, eager to give permission but not money. It seemed that he was willing to let the rich merchants take the risk of exploration while he took all the credit. Still another explanation is that in the late 1400s, England was not yet the world power she would later become under the reign of King Henry VIII (1509–1547) and still later under the leadership of Elizabeth I (1558–1603). Without much confidence of bringing England greater claim to Asia, Henry VII made a very small official investment in Cabot's second trip.

Business records from the Bristol archives indicate that merchants financed four additional ships. Although they had viewed Cabot's maps and seen or heard of maps made of Columbus's voyages, Cabot's business partners may not have been convinced by either explorer that the lands they had encountered were, in fact, the shores of Asia. Without greater evidence that the Spice Islands of Asia were within reach, these businessmen, like their king, would not, and perhaps could not, invest any more money

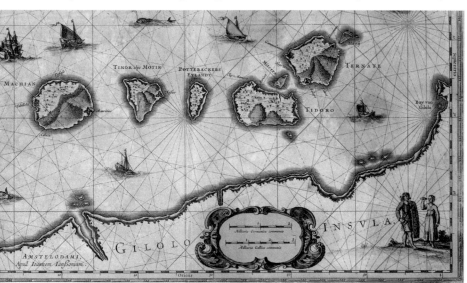

Many investors were suspicious of Cabot's discoveries. Without proof that Cabot had landed on the Asian Spice Islands (above), many refused to invest more than a little in his second voyage.

in Cabot's voyage. Cabot, once a poor man, apparently had no riches of his own that he wished to invest in the journey. The yearly pension that Henry VII had granted him in August 1497 was not paid until early 1498. Though it was enough to improve his lifestyle and allow him to live well, it was not the sort of wealth necessary to purchase and outfit a sailing ship. Still, Cabot's five ships were more than Columbus's first three, but less than the fleet of fifteen that Columbus took on his second voyage to the West Indies.

Setting Sail Again

With five ships committed to his venture, Cabot put to sea in early May 1498. As recorded in the official *Chronicles of London*, the ships carried with them many goods suitable for trading, such as cloth, lace, and wool.

Cabot chose to follow the same route in 1498 that he had taken in 1497. He sailed from Bristol to the southwestern coast of Ireland and may have followed the 51 degrees north line of latitude westward to Newfoundland. Unfortunately, Cabot's second voyage, however well supplied, was destined for complete failure.

Pedro de Ayala, Spain's junior ambassador to England, wrote to his sovereigns Ferdinand and Isabella in July 1498 that "news has come that one of these, in which sailed another Friar Buil, has made land in Ireland in a great storm with the ship badly damaged. The Genoese [Cabot] kept on his way."

Soon after the five ships set sail from Ireland a great storm hit. One ship turned back, while the others, with Cabot among those on board, continued the journey, but no other mention of him or the fleet was made again. For centuries, people thought the small fleet was apparently lost at sea. Official records, personal letters, and even history books written in the mid-1500s do not tell the story of what happened to Cabot or to the others on board those four large ships. The admiral's dreams of riches, as well as his dreams of a place in history, ended abruptly.

Cabot's name appears again in England's records, but in a confusing array of locations. Polydore Vergil, an Italian priest who became an English citizen and close friend of King Henry VII, wrote of the explorer's voyages and tragic death in his famous histories of England in 1512–1513, a chronicle that was later published in 1534. The published versions of Vergil's history do not include Cabot's name, but notes on the document, preserved in the Vatican library in Rome, show the name "Ioanne Cabot" inserted in spaces that Vergil had left blank. That suggests to some that as little as fifteen years after his successful crossing of the Atlantic, people had already forgotten about the explorer.

Recently however, a different theory of the result of Cabot's final journey has emerged. Dr. Alwyn Ruddock was a historian who researched and studied the life and work of Cabot for more than half her life. Her research suggested that Cabot's final journey was successful. She discovered that on board Cabot's five ships were a number of Italian friars looking to build a religious colony in the New World. Among those friars was Cabot's former ally Carbonariis. The friars were delivered to the coast of Newfoundland, and Cabot sailed down the eastern coast of North America, claiming it all for the British. After an encounter with one of Columbus's captains near South America, Cabot returned to Newfoundland in 1500. He later sailed back to Bristol, where he died a few months after his return. Ruddock died before she could publish her planned book on Cabot. A team of researchers associated with the Cabot Project, an international effort created in 2009 to further study Cabot's journeys, are continuing Ruddock's work in discovering what truly became of Cabot.

Chapter 6

England and the New World

Even with the hard work of Ruddock and the Cabot Project, much is still left unknown about Cabot's life and journeys. Historians continue to piece together what they can based on official documents from a variety of sources. From the records of

John Cabot is memorialized in this statue located in Bristol, England, the point from which he began his journey to North America.

John Cabot

King Henry VII, it is known that a pension payment addressed to Cabot was made in 1498, suggesting that Cabot returned to England after his second journey to the New World. However, some believe that the payment may not have been made to Cabot himself but to his wife.

Rent on Cabot's home in Bristol was also received sometime in late 1498, but again, no one knows precisely who paid that bill.

Cabot may have once again reached the shores of Newfoundland. Only one ship returned to Ireland after encountering the rough storm. The other four may have continued onward. In 1501, the Venetian ambassador in Portugal wrote a letter to his brother in Venice. According to James Williamson in *The Cabot Voyages*, the letter described the homecoming of Gaspar Corte Real, a Portuguese explorer who sailed the eastern coast of the North American continent in 1500. "These men have brought from there a piece of broken gilt sword, which certainly seems to have been made in Italy. One of the boys was wearing in his ears two silver rings which without doubt seem to have been made in Venice," the letter stated.

These artifacts have suggested to some historians that Cabot, or at least members of his 1498 expedition, did actually reach the shores of Newfoundland. Other historians argue that any sailors traveling from any European port to the New World could have left those artifacts behind, including Cabot during his first voyage.

No one served as a spokesperson for Cabot to tell of his explorations, as did Ferdinand Columbus, son of Christopher, who wrote a biography of his father. In many ways, uncontrollable fates effectively prevented generations of people who looked back on Cabot's accomplishments from seeing clearly, or faintly, his contribution to Europe's influence over North and South America.

The Significance of Cabot's Journeys

With such little historical evidence regarding Cabot, scholars have proposed theories about hidden events that may explain the uneven historical record that does survive.

James Williamson suggests that soon after Cabot's voyage of 1498, perhaps even as a result of it, England's royalty and members of its wealthy upper class underwent a change of thought regarding the "new found land" that Cabot had explored. Official documents in the king's records, including letters, record books, and preserved discussions of the westward adventures of explorers and merchants, no longer referred to Cipango, Cathay, or the dream of reaching Asia by a shorter ocean route. Still, even if England knew that Cabot had not reached Asia, the explorer may have died without realizing this himself.

Cabot's explorations paved the way for the founding of Jamestown, the first permanent English colony in North America.

Cabot's dream of a westerly ocean voyage to Asia seemed to fade from discussion, replaced by the realization that a continent lay between England and Asia. Less than ten years after Cabot's successful voyage, records refer to a "new found land" as a continent and a barrier in their efforts to reach Asia. By the very early 1500s, explorers, including Cabot's son Sebastian, had begun seeking a Northwest Passage through this new land to those Asian riches.

Though his dream did not come true, Cabot's voyage of 1497 was an important event in England's history. With his stories, maps, globes, and the testimony of his crew, he revealed the existence of a land no more than 2,000 miles (3,219 km) to the west.

It took more than a century for Cabot's discovery to become significant to England's efforts to colonize the New World. Though explorations continued, it was not until 1607 that England established Jamestown, its first official settlement in the New World, except for the failed Roanoke colony, in what would later become the state of Virginia.

Historians suggest that the most valuable contribution of Cabot's journey was that it gave England a basis to stake a claim to the lands in the New World. King Henry VII and his son, Henry VIII, did not act aggressively upon the potential of that new land, but without the king's participation in the venture, England would have been weakened in its competition with Spain, Portugal, and France in laying any claim to new lands on distant shores.

Conflicts in Europe between England and its rivals slowed efforts of exploration, but Cabot's voyage paved the way for a century of discovery of the shores of Labrador, Newfoundland, Nova Scotia, and Maine. Indeed, Sebastian Cabot is credited by some historians with having explored Hudson Bay in Canada in

1509, almost 100 years before English navigator Henry Hudson, for whom it is named, did so.

Cabot's successful voyage had proved to England that tremendously rich fishing waters lay less than a month's journey across the Atlantic Ocean. Twentieth-century archaeologists and historians have suggested that these waters, with their ample supplies of cod, motivated Bristol's merchants to continue financing fishing fleets to harvest the fish for the wealth it brought.

RUDDOCK'S LOST BOOK

One of the great scholarly opportunities in understanding the history of John Cabot's life was lost in 2005 with the passing of Dr. Alwyn Ruddock. For more than a decade, Ruddock had been working on a book on Cabot's life to be published by University of Exeter Press. However, she never finished the book to her satisfaction, and upon her death, she left specific instructions for her research to be destroyed. Why she made this choice is a mystery almost as tantalizing as Cabot's final journey itself. However, researchers trying to recreate her work have so far found her assertions were correct, particularly that Cabot did have the financial backing of an Italian bank for his journeys, when most assumed that only British interests had bankrolled him. Time will tell if her additional claims that his final voyage was successful and not the failure history has assumed it was will prove true as well.

Unanswered Questions

Five hundred years after his voyage to the New World, John Cabot remains an intriguing mystery. Some people, in fact, claim that Cabot is one of history's greatest forgotten heroes.

Writers have hailed Cabot as the man who contributed more to the wealth of England than any other explorer. He returned to England from one brief journey with knowledge of a land that

Cabot's Tower, located in St. John's, Newfoundland and Labrador, Canada, was built on the 400th anniversary of Cabot's discovery.

lay just a short voyage across the ocean to the west. In the name of one small island nation, England, Cabot laid claim to a vast continent.

King Henry VII may have been disappointed that he did not find a westerly passage to Asia. Over the course of history, however, Cabot's voyages and the flags he planted on behalf of England gave that country the beginning it needed to build a stronger kingdom.

Today, colleges in Canada are named after Cabot. The people of Newfoundland, Nova Scotia, and English-speaking Canada view this Venetian merchant as the true European discoverer of North America. Though Cabot has never been commemorated in Canada as Columbus has been in the United States, Canadians take pride in the one voyage of this sailor who introduced England to a new world of riches.

In 1997, Cabot enthusiasts sailed this replica of the *Matthew* from Bristol, England, to Newfoundland, Canada, keeping the memory of the mysterious explorer alive.

In the late 1800s, the English port city of Bristol built a monument to Cabot, a 150-foot (46 meter) tower that stands on Brandon Hill and overlooks the city. In 1997, Cabot enthusiasts set sail across the Atlantic Ocean in a recreation of the *Matthew*'s journey. They followed Cabot's presumed route to Newfoundland, maintained life on board as Cabot and his crew would have done, and took exactly as many days to reach the mainland. A replica of the *Matthew* now resides at Bristol's docks. Guests may venture aboard the ship and even join the crew as they take her on short ocean tours.

Cabot's journey has been hard to recreate. Anyone concerned with retelling it accurately must struggle with a scarce supply of original documents and too little information. None have been able to bring Cabot's story into clear focus. In fact, even visual artists over the centuries have had to turn to their own imaginations to paint and sculpt portraits of the explorer because no images of him have survived.

With the tireless efforts of the Cabot Project and other researchers, the hope is that information will eventually come to light that answers all the remaining questions about John Cabot. Despite these loose ends, the significance of Cabot's journey cannot be doubted. Cabot changed the course of history with his discovery, and earned an important place in the history of European exploration of the New World.

Timeline

985

Erik the Red sails west from Iceland, discovering Greenland.

circa 1000

Approximate year that Erik the Red's son, Leif Eriksson, sails to present-day Newfoundland in North America.

1298

Marco Polo writes about his travels to Asia, exciting Europeans about the riches there.

circa 1450

Probable year of John Cabot's birth.

1453

Constantinople falls to the Turks and sparks interest in new trade routes to the East.

1480s

English merchant ships sail throughout the waters of the Atlantic Ocean, possibly as far west as North America.

1492

Christopher Columbus, sponsored by the Spanish crown, discovers the West Indies.

1494

The Treaty of Tordesillas divides the discoveries of the New World between Spain and Portugal with an imaginary line from the North Pole to the South Pole.

1495

Cabot, his wife, and their three sons move to the seaport town of Bristol, England.

1495–96

Cabot petitions King Henry VII of England for financial support to sail to the New World.

1497

Cabot sails to Newfoundland, Canada, under England's flag.

1498

Vasco da Gama finds a new trade route to India by sailing around the coast of Africa. Records of Cabot's second voyage are lost, and Cabot is lost at sea and presumed dead.

1499

Amerigo Vespucci explores the South American coastline.

1507

Sebastian Cabot sails to North America. The first map is printed naming North and South America after Vespucci.

1519–1522

Ferdinand Magellan circumnavigates the globe.

1607

Jamestown, the first permanent settlement of the English in the New World, is founded.

1992

Dr. Alwyn Ruddock, an expert in the life of John Cabot, agrees to publish a book theorizing Cabot's last voyage was actually successful. Ruddock dies in 2005 before completing her book, and her research is destroyed per her request.

Glossary

astrolabe A navigator's tool used to determine latitude.

Brasil The mythical Isle of Brasil, a legendary island far to the west of England in the Atlantic Ocean; also a term often found on European maps made before 1500 to designate unknown islands in the distant Atlantic Ocean.

cartographer A person who works with or makes maps and/or charts.

Cathay An old European name for China, often used during the Middle Ages and the Renaissance.

Cipango A mysterious island of medieval European legend believed to lie east of Asia; generally identified in modern times as Japan.

city-state An independent city that is itself a separate nation. Venice and Genoa were powerful city-states during the Middle Ages and the Renaissance.

cross-staff An instrument for measuring the angle of elevation of heavenly bodies. It was made of a long rod, or staff, calibrated in degrees. A shorter second rod, perpendicular to the first, slid up and down the long rod. It was used to measure latitude by determining the position of the North Star.

dominion A territory that is governed; having absolute owner-ship over something.

dowry The property given to a husband from his wife's family.

exchequer Under the English government system, the depart-ment responsible for the country's revenue.

Genoa A present-day city in northwestern Italy on the Ligurian Sea. In the 1500s, Genoa was a powerful city-state and leading commercial center.

league In navigational terms, a unit of measure equaling about three miles in English-speaking countries. However, the length of a league has varied over time and across nations, making the determination of the exact distance difficult.

log A ship's official record of events during its voyage.

Milan Located in northern Italy, Milan was a powerful city and seat of the duchy (a region ruled by a duke). Milan serves as capital of the region of Lombardy.

monarch The hereditary ruler of a nation that follows a governmental structure; a king or queen.

patent letter A public or open letter granting rights or privileges to someone; an official document or contract.

patronage The support and encouragement of a wealthy sponsor—often in the form of money—given to a person with talent and skills who does not have the wealth to be self-supporting.

quadrant A navigational instrument used for measuring latitude, consisting of a quarter circle, marked in degrees, and a moveable rod for aligning with the North Star.

Simancas A city of ancient origins in north central Spain.

Venetian A person from Venice, a city in northeastern Italy on the Adriatic Sea. In the 1500s, Venice was an extensive city-state, governing much of the surrounding lands.

For More Information

Books

Garfield, Henry. *The Lost Voyage of John Cabot*. New York, NY: Atheneum Books for Young Readers, 2010.

Hunter, Douglas. *The Race to the New World: Christopher Columbus, John Cabot, and a Lost History of Discovery*. New York, NY: Palgrave Macmillan, 2011.

McCoy, Roger. *On the Edge: Mapping North America's Coasts*. New York, NY: Oxford University Press, 2012.

Ober, Frederick Albion. *John and Sebastian Cabot—Primary Source Edition*. Charleston, SC: Nabu Press, 2013.

Websites

The History Channel, "John Cabot"
www.history.com/topics/exploration/john-cabot
The History Channel's page on John Cabot provides a brief biography of the explorer and features numerous videos related to Cabot and the Age of Exploration.

The Mariner's Museum: Giovanni Caboto (John Cabot)
ageofex.marinersmuseum.org/index.php?type=explorer&id=74
Learn more about the life of John Cabot and accounts of his voyages. View photos and read the history of ships used by Egyptian, Phoenician, and Dutch explorers.

The University of Bristol's Cabot Project Web Page
www.bristol.ac.uk/history/research/cabot
Investigate the Bristol discovery voyages of the late fifteenth and sixteenth centuries, particularly the fate of Cabot's final journey.

Index